Urban Warfare

The invasion and occupation of African American Communities

By

Lawrence Hutton

ISBN: 978-0-578-91399-5

TABLE OF CONTENT

Chapter 1

Urban Warfare

Every day we turn on our Televisions to see conflict and war anytime across the globe, in just about every Nation in the world. Gone are the days of World Wars and even the days of Jungle Warfare. Today's battles are being fought in residential and city environments in what is now called ***Urban Warfare***. Urban Warfare is military combat set in urban and residential regions of mostly civilian populated areas. In Urban Warfare the invading forces are restricted from using heavy equipment such as tanks and artillery. In a Global War there are lines drawn on the battlefield i.e., the front. In Urban Warfare there are no front lines. A skirmish can happen anywhere at anytime. Urban battles are what is known as ***Close Quarters Combat,*** in which soldiers are fighting in the streets and house to house. During these engagements, the Combatants must take into consideration the civilians and the terrain.

Military combat operations are conducted daily to maintain operational and tactical readiness. During these operations Intelligence is gathered, and surveillance is conducted. Strength, size, and equipment of the opposing force is taken to be used in future operations. As these conflicts continue around the world there are always advancements in training and technology. Times have change and it continues to change; this is now a world of Urban Warfare.

During each encounter, in each engagement, information is gathered on what, when, why, and how it all happened. This information is then studied to see if the operation could be conducted better or more efficiently. Tactics that are used in actual combat are being used by Law Enforcement in urban areas in the United States. We are now known as an Urban Species. As of 2008, 50% of the world has become urban. It is projected that by 2060 75% of the world will be urban. Apart from Africa most of the world is already in an urban posture. The globe is in Urbanization.

As Urban Warfare training is conducted throughout the world. Mock Urban areas are created to help simulate actual Urban encounters with realistic training, so that soldiers know how to shoot and move in an Urban Warfare environment. So why am I talking about this? Because todays Law Enforcement has become Paramilitary. Since the 911 attacks more Law Enforcement Agencies have turned to military training and equipment as well as learning Close Quarter Combat. Look around, in just about every city Law Enforcement agencies have become militarized, especially in African American urban areas where police presence has grown. Law Enforcement Officers in those area look no different than some soldiers in other countries. If you look at what is going on in the U.S. it is happening right here in our own neighborhoods the same way U.S. Soldiers are occupying third world countries, Law Enforcement is occupying our predominantly black urban neighborhoods. The government says it is for the protection of the civilians but if you stand back and really look at what is going on here and in third world countries with check points which stops everyone who comes in and out of neighborhoods. They are identified and questioned. So, what we see is a large police presence. Cameras and Drones are used for surveillance on every activity that goes on in black neighborhoods. But the funny thing is you do not, nor will you see them in predominantly white residential or white urban areas of the country.

A tactic used by those running this operation is the divide and conquer tactics that goes back to the times of Machiavelli and Caesar. The elements of this technique involve creating or encouraging division among subjects and alliances aiding and promoting those who are willing to cooperate. Fostering distrust and enmity. These tactics can cause damage beyond believe and beyond repair. We have allowed these tactics to go on way to long. We have allowed a wedge to be driven between African American families as well. It was meant for African American Men and Women to be a couple, a team.

We were put here to work together not to constantly go at each other with a lot of nonsense about who is stronger, whose smarter, black women are Gold Diggers black men are dogs. This mental joust between black men and women needs to be put to a halt. Stop allowing others to create the perception of African Americans. We need to stop being divided by the battle of the sexes. There are great Women and Men, Bitches and Mother Fuckers. It is not about who is the better gender it is about the personality and intelligence. Both Men and Women have strengths and weaknesses. It is on the Man to know his Woman's weakness and step up and help her where she falls short. The same goes for a Woman, to know and understand her man and help him with his short comings.

This will make the house a home and to have each other to lean on in good times and bad. We need to walk away from these surveys and turn off these talk shows about Men versus Women. We are two different sexes so how and why are we comparing or competing? It is literally apples and oranges. This is how we are being divided. Back when women where fighting for equal rights. The powers that be, allowed Women to have equal rights, not because it was the right thing to do, but because it created more taxpayers.

Back then one paycheck took care of everything and it was that check that got taxed. There is only a small group of black role models that the African American adults must set the examples for the younger generation and look to those who could be considered a true leader. There are some young women being brain washed by other black women to believe they do not need a man. A woman can raise a boy to be an adult, but a woman cannot raise a boy to be a man, and young men should not think they do not need a woman, just get the right woman. This also effects our children.

They look at how their mother and father treat each other and take what they see as normal behavior. If a girl sees her mother being abused by her father and their mother does nothing about it, then the girl will date abusive men when she gets older. If a son sees their father abuse his mother and his mother puts up with it then he will grow up to be an abusive man. There is also a cultural attack on our children. The attack on our children are the worst because it is attacking our future generation, while they are young in hopes to get them indoctrinated by those who are in charge into how they will be in the future. To be the ***"Sheeple"*** of the future, the ones that just allows themselves to be led around by their nose rings. We have an educational system that tells our children if your parents put their hands on you call the police.

Now yes there are times when police need to be called for abuse but not corporal punishment. There is a difference between abuse and discipline. Children will use that “Call the Police” to get out of being disciplined. There are those western cultured Clinical Psychologists who tell us how to raise black children and some do not even have children of their own and if they do, some of their children are train wrecks, or if you sat down with their children, they would probably tell you how their parents are never home nor even spend time with them because they are so caught up in the careers. Some of the time their either dealing with a pregnant or heroin addict daughter or a heroin addict and or alcoholic son. But they tell us how to raise our children. All the while coming up with this idea of allowing children to have free thought. They are children, they are too young to have free thought, they are still in the learning years of age. Free thought should not be taught until 13-14 years old as their minds start to mature. There is also the dumbing down of our school system.

They are teaching our children how to take a test but not really teaching them how to think. This **No child left behind** is insane. What the educational system is doing is pushing our children through school and giving them a certificate of completion when they are done. They release them into society and expect them to make it on their own in a world that has turned HI-TECH. But those who are imposing this method on our children have their children going to private schools and or Vocational Schools. Our children are being setup for failure because of the poor-quality education.

The 19th century congress passed the 1878 Posse Comitatus Act because of the alleged abuse under the former Confederate States by members of the United States Military. The Law prevents the United States Military from being used as domestic Law Enforcement except when authorized by the President. In the 1930's the FBI and Kansas City Police authorized the use of the Browning automatic rifle by Law Enforcement Officers and Agents. Fast forward to 1950-1960 Police militarization was born, the success of stopping the race riots in Watts with military weapons started the trend of arming and equipping Law Enforcement with battlefield weapon.

Joy Rohde began a study "The origins of modern militarized policing". There are those who believe the reason for the explosion of military hardware to Law Enforcement was the War on Drugs and the War on Terror. During the Regan administration in 1981 was the birth of The Military Cooperation with civilian Law Enforcement Agency act. Public Law 97-86 Title 10 Chapter 8 is the government authorization to transfer all types of military equipment available. The 1033 Program transfer all excess military equipment to Law Enforcement.

"The Insurrection Act of 1807 is a United States federal law that governs the ability of the President of the United States to deploy military troops within the United States to put down lawlessness, insurrection, and rebellion. The general purpose is to limit presidential power, relying on state and local governments for initial response in the event of insurrection. Coupled with the Posse Comitatus Act, presidential powers for domestic law enforcement are limited and delayed."

-Wikipedia

Chapter 2

All-out War

One of the many operations of a military is Intelligence gathering and surveillance. This is done, using current technology to monitor communications and aerial and video monitoring. In current military operations for surveillance and visual observation is the Drone. This piece of hardware was used in the Gulf War and other prior military engagements. Now this is being adopted and used by Law Enforcement in urban regions of the United States. Everything we say, write and or post in video form is being watched examined, recorded, and documented. Everything is scrubbed through a system of algorithms looking for certain key words. Its then that you get the attention of certain agencies. Eric Blair, known to us all as George Orwell. An English Journalist and who was best known for his novel 1984.

He wrote about the same terms that are used today i.e., Big Brother, Thought Police, and Doublethink. The term Doublethink is when one is accepting two contradictory ideas at the same time. A man before his time we also coin the term Orwellian for the fact that we see some of his ideas that he wrote about coming to past as we speak. One of these agencies that are looking at us is the FBI. Between the 1956 and 1971 there was a covert program called **COINTELPRO.**

***CO**-**Intel**ligence –**Pro**gram*

These covert projects were conducted at the time on Civil Rights Groups.

The Civil Rights Movement

The Black Power Movement

The Nation of Islam

The Black Panther Party

Dr. Martin Luther King Jr.

The FBI used 5 COINTELPRO.

Infiltration

Psychological Warfare

Harassment via the legal system

Illegal Force

Undermine Public option

J. Edgar Hoover

The FBI, under J. Edgar Hoover declared war on the African Americans like no other individual since the KKK. While under J. Edgar Hoover, the FBI launch the COINTELPRO program which African American Men and Black Organizations were its main targets under Hoover and the Federal Government. The FBI also conducted an operation called ***"Operation Fruehmenschen"*** Which is German for ***Primitive Man.*** There was a report stemming from an article ***"The Dilemma of Black Politics"*** by Dr. Mary Sawyer.

Here is a portion of what the report consisted of:

"I found a pattern of harassment of black officials," said Sawyer, whose 10-year-old study, "The Dilemma of Black Politics," written for the National Association of Human Rights Workers, is soon to be updated. "I believe the harassment issue is real today."

Why do whites harass black politicians? In the 265-page report, Sawyer found that position and political philosophy played a role.

The highest black elected official in a given jurisdiction was often "the more probable target" for harassment, which she found ranged from anonymous death threats to "unfair media treatment" and selective prosecution.

Sawyer stressed that neither her old study nor her follow-up claims that wrongdoing or corruption among black officials did not exist, but that "the scrutiny . . . is more intense, that investigations are pursued on the basis of less evidence, that stories are printed with less solid information so there is an inequity in how black officials are treated as opposed to how white officials are treated."

The FBI's ***BLACKLIST*** consisted of:

Philip Randolph: Vice President of the AFL-CIO and outspoken black leader.

National Negro Congress

Adam Clayton Powell: NYC Council in 1945

The Black Panther Party

The NAACP

Elijah Muhammad

Malcolm X

The Organization of Afro-American Unity

The Reverend Jesse Jackson

Roy Wilkins: Member of the NAACP

Thurgood Marshall

W. E. B. Du Bois

Marcus Garvey

To name a few....

UNITED STATES GOVERNMENT

Memorandum

DECLASSIFIED
Authority: ED 60537
By: NARA Date

TO : SAC, Albany

DATE: 10/9/68

FROM : Director, FBI (157-8415)

SUBJECT: BLACK NATIONALIST MOVEMENT IN THE UNITED STATES
RACIAL MATTERS
BUDED: 11/8/68

The Bureau has noted an increase in the establishment of black extremist bookstores which represent propaganda outlets for revolutionary and hate publications and cultural centers for extremism. Each office should locate and identify black extremist and/or African-type bookstores in its territory and open separate discreet investigations on each to determine if it is extremist in nature. Advise under this caption by 11/8/68 of the investigations instituted in accordance with these instructions.

The investigation should determine the identities of the owners; whether it is a front for any group or foreign interest; whether individuals affiliated with the store engage in extremist activities; the number, type, and source of books and material on sale; the store's financial condition; its clientele; and whether it is used as a headquarters or meeting place. Submit results under individual caption in form suitable for dissemination along with a recommendation as to whether additional investigation is warranted.

Investigations should be instituted on new stores when opened and you should recognize the excellent target these stores represent for penetration by racial sources.

2 - All Offices

157-368-80

SCREENED
By Date

SEARCHED INDEXED
SERIALIZED FILED
OCT 11 1968
FBI — WASH. F. O.

Buy U.S. Savings Bonds Regularly on the Payroll Savings Plan

This memo was sent from the J. Edgar Hoover to investigate all black owned bookstores.

It is unknown why there were never any major investigations or reports on the Ku Klux Klan and its leaders, Grand Dragons, i.e., why is that? History tells that the Klan was born in 1871 and no investigation, no reports, and yet no documents. The federal government began its surveillance of blacks and civil rights leaders in 1917 starting with Marcus Garvey. Garvey appeared on the radar of J. Edgar Hoover in 1919 labeling him **"The Notorious Negro Agitator".** Hoover then had black informants infiltrate Garvey's Universal Negro Improvement Association which was at that time the largest black organization in history. After using a black undercover FBI agent, Hoover was able to dismantle the black owned shipping line operation and sent Garvey to prison for mail fraud. With that victory Hoover used these same tactics on black civil rights leaders, another one was Martin Luther King. There are some who looked at Hoover as Captain Ahab and King was Moby Dick. The Black Panthers were born in1966, 95 years later and yet the FBI has a storage shed filled with reports on the Panthers. The FBI also obtains intelligence from something as simple as Census Data.

The FBI uses this information to map Communities by race and ethnicity and to identify and monitor ethnic facilities and behaviors. The FBI office in Atlanta Ga. used this data and claimed that the information showed a possible Black Separatist Terrorism Threat was imminent. This imminent threat was justification which allowed the FBI to initiate a threat assessment. In 2008 the FBI introduced a program called ***Assessments,*** once the FBI has determined what person or organization is a threat and insert the necessary verbiage to create the narrative of fear, they have their investigation, this assessment is conducted for 30 days. If necessary, the Agent can request, through a Supervisor, to extend the assessment for another 30 days.

We must be very aware on what is going on here. They are still applying the same force against African Americans but now it is under a different name and why these reports are only being initiated after an incident of physical or deadly force is used by Law Enforcement on African Americans the FBI starts to monitor any possible violent retaliation by Africa Americans. The FBI started its campaign using COINTELPRO which once reviled was ended in the 1970's, now it's the Counter Terrorist Reports starting in 2017 named **IRON FIST.** On these reports the Black Identity Extremists and Black Lives Matter are now re-classified as terrorist. There are other systems and devices used by the Government and Law Enforcement to monitor and or detect communications by civilians. One of these devices is known as an IMSI catcher (INTERNATIONAL MOBILE SUBSCRIBER IDENTITY CATCHER) used to intercept and track a mobile device. This device acts like a Cell Phone tower which deceives the Cell Phone thinking it is communicating with a real communications tower.

An Intelligence Assessment report was written by the FBI and acquired by the ACLU. In this report it tells how and what types of investigations the FBI have been conducting on the African American Culture. The Department of Homeland Security also participates in this intelligence collection. On March of 2018 racial justice organizations files a Civil Suit against DHS to release documents that Department of Homeland Security dubbed the "Race Papers".

The Honorable Kirstjen Nielsen
Secretary of Homeland Security
Washington, DC 20528
May 30, 2018
Dear Secretary Nielsen:

The undersigned civil rights and civil liberties groups call for the release of the un-redacted
Memo referred to in Department of Homeland Security Office of Intelligence and Analysis
documents as the "Race Paper" and "Growing Frequency of Race-Related Domestic Terrorist
violence. DHS intelligence and threat analysis inform the activities of law enforcement
officials at all levels of government. Thus, we are concerned that biases and inaccuracies
reflected in the "Race Paper" could result in unconstitutional law enforcement activities
throughout the country that disproportionately impact activists, protesters, and communities of
color. The Race Paper's existence came to light recently as part of a Freedom of Information Act (FOIA) request, but the document itself was released in entirely redacted form.3 However,

DHS's recently filed declaration indicates that the document was intended to survey growing trends in domestic terrorism driven by race-related "extremist" ideologies and address the coopting of peaceful protests by violent ideological actors.

The declaration also reveals that DHS believes it has identified common indicators displayed by those engaging in domestic terrorism. Given what the declaration reveals about DHS's focus on racial identity as it relates to domestic terrorism, we believe that the Race Paper may improperly suggest that constitutionally protected Black political speech should be considered an indicator of criminal conduct or a national security threat. A flawed analysis of this type would raise troubling questions about DHS's priorities, resource allocations, and intelligence methodologies. It would also have serious implications on the constitutional rights and safety of Black and Brown people in the United States, and protesters and activists of color. The U.S. government has a long history of monitoring activists of color.5 For instance, during the Civil Rights Movement, federal law enforcement tried to suppress political dissent by targeting Black organizations and leadership through a range of illegal activities under the auspices of the COINTELPRO program. That program and other efforts to survey Black communities are now seen as a stain on the history of federal law enforcement and resulted in robust reforms meant to protect against similar future abuses. However, recent reports of police tracking the movements and affiliations of Black and Brown anti-racist protesters represent a chilling continuation of this shameful history.

Other recently released documents, such as the Federal Bureau of Investigation's "Black Identity Extremist" report, show federal law enforcement is developing race-based analysis to justify targeting and surveilling protesters of color with unjustified and unconstitutional scrutiny. These documents wrongly characterize peaceful, anti-racist groups carrying out First Amendment-protected activity as having a propensity for violence and therefore worthy of invasive and persistent surveillance. Similar to the FBI documents, DHS's declaration mentions that the "Race Paper" examines peaceful protests that have been co-opted by violent "extremists." But there is no evidence that Black racial justice and anti-police brutality activism has been co-opted in such a manner. DHS has stated that releasing the document would cause public confusion. We disagree. The public has a right to know whether the Department is improperly using race or constitutionally protected political activity as an indicator of violent behavior. Withholding the documents only contributes to lack of public trust and confidence in the Department.

We demand that DHS's "Race Paper" be released immediately. Given our country's long history of discriminatory policing, the public should not be left to speculate about the content and insinuations hidden in this document.

Sincerely,

American Civil Liberties Union
Arab American Institute
Brennan Center for Justice
Campaign for Liberty
Campaign for Youth Justice
Center for Democracy & Technology
Center for Media Justice
Color of Change
Defending Rights and Dissent
Demand Progress Action
18MillionRising.org
Electronic Frontier Foundation
Free Press
Free Speech Coalition
Government Information Watch
Human Rights Watch
Juvenile Justice Coalition (Ohio)
Law for Black Lives – DC
Lawyers' Committee for Civil Rights Under Law
Media Freedom Foundation

MPower Change
Muslim Advocates
Muslim Justice League
(Continued)

NAACP
National Association of Criminal Defense Lawyers
National Coalition Against Censorship
National Hispanic Media Coalition
National Immigration Law Center
National Juvenile Justice Network
National Lawyers Guild
National LGBTQ Task Force
New America's Open Technology Institute
New Jersey Parents' Caucus
PEN America
Project Censored
Restore The Fourth
The Center on Privacy and Technology at Georgetown Law
The Constitution Project at POGO
The Southern Poverty Law Center
United Congregations of Metro East (Illinois)
Woodhull Freedom Foundation
X-Lab

So, in the FBI report regarding Black Identity Extremist (BIE). There are issues with those who plot against Law Enforcement and or the Government, but as you read their report it states that these groups are created only when there is an incident where an African American is killed by a Law Enforcement Officer. Now if that is the case then these groups and or factions are not the cause but the effect when a black person is killed by Law Enforcement. The report does not read anything about coming together to overthrow a government or start an insurrection against the United States. These groups and every other group from the Black Panthers to the NAACP were created to fight and conquer social injustice in this county that has plagued the African American Culture since time and remembrance. It seems to be a fear felt by Western Culture of any type of retaliation by African Americans regardless of if it is only against an injustice.

I believe Stokely Carmichael said it best in a speech he gave on a Greek Theatre Campus in 1966

"This country is too hypocritical, and we cannot adjust ourselves to its hypocrisy. White people beat up Black people every day, do not nobody talk about nonviolence. But as soon as Black people start to move, the double standard comes into being. You can't defend yourself that's what you're saying."

There is an Organization called "We the People" who are online white supremist. After doing some research on the internet, I find that it has "Dog Whistle" words of the old Make America Great Again slogan which also takes one back to the old times and the ways of Jim Crow that ***"GREAT AGAIN"*** part. As to say America was always great and we need to go back there, to slavery, segregation, and Jim Crow. This group***, "We the People"*** filed a petition to the United States Government to have Black Lives Matters be placed on the Terrorist List. And of course, the Government denied the request. But this group managed to obtain 140,000 votes from white supporters. And the words "restore our bill of rights" and "Gather all the Patriots" is all reminiscent of slavery and bondage. Even the names they give themselves....

American Freedom Party

Proud Boys

Assembly of Christian Soldiers

Citizens Councils

White Patriot Party

MISSION STATEMENT

Our mission is to save America. The country of and for "We the people". Restore our "Bill of rights". In doing so maintain "Life, liberty and the pursuit of happiness".
Step 1; Gather all the Patriots!

ABOUT US

Prior to the organization "We the People" being formed, there was another organization called the White Citizens' Council (WCC). This organization was form in 1954 shortly after Brown vs the Board of Education. This group consisted of middle-class and upper-class whites who not only used violence but sought to oppress blacks economically and socially. The White Citizens Council was supported by J. Edgar Hoover and other members of the United States Government during the Hoover administration. Unlike the KKK, the White Citizens Council met in the open. It carried the ideology of the KKK but acted like the Rotary Club. The Council went from producing the newsletters ***The Citizens Council*** by 1961 they were producing the magazine until 1989 called ***The Citizen.***

CITIZENS' COUNCILS
STATES' RIGHTS · RACIAL INTEGRITY

This booklet was written by Judge Tom P. Brady of the 4th Circuit Court District of Brookhaven, Mississippi. Judge Brady was also a member to the White Citizens Council. In his booklet Brady writes,

"Those are things we can see. We do not know what happens to the brain of man. But we do know that the Negro's brain pan seal and hardens quicker than the white men. We do know the Negro has, in certain instances, elliptical blood cells, which causes disease. We do know that his skull is one-eighth inch thicker, and we do know he has to have two determiners to have his kinky black hair. We don't know what it takes to make his mind different from our mind."

This booklet speaks on the reasons that blacks should not be integrated with white children because blacks are inferior and against the will of God. White Citizens Council (WCC), after 1956 was renamed Citizens Councils of America with over 60,000 members across the United States. The Citizens Councils in 1963 pushed a public challenge Law allowing 2 voters to challenge another to see if he was registered. A Law used to purge the rolls of black voters, in one location ***Benville Parish*** 95% of black voters were purged and in Louisiana It was ***Voter Qualification Laws.*** As of March 27, 2021 the Georgia State Government passed a Law hindering voter registration this would affect the African American community in that state indefinitely. After the Federal Civil Rights Legislation, the Organization disappeared and then rear appeared in 1985 as the Council of Conservative Citizens a

Non-Governmental-Organization (NGO). The Citizens Councils, whose primary mission was to keep segregation and prevent the mixing of races. To keep things status quo, the Council used violent forms of intimidation. This came in the form of Lynching, Shootings, Rapes and Arson. State and Local Politicians were also members. Then the organization again changed their name to ***The State Sovereignty Commission.*** It gives one the idea that these Proud Boys, KKK, White Supremacist, Neo Nazis are nothing more that Loyalist to the United States Government. The Council also formed and continued to hold private segregation academies out of the reach of the ruling public.

July 16th of 1956 the Louisiana State Legislature passed a law mandating racial segregation signed into law by Governor Earl Long which went into effect October 15th, 1956.

The act read in part:

An Act to prohibit all interracial dancing, social functions, entertainments, athletic training, games, sports, or contests and other such activities; to provide for separate seating and other facilities for white and negroes... That all persons, firms, and corporations are prohibited from sponsoring, arranging, participating in, or permitting on premises under their control ... such activities involving personal and social contact in which the participants are members of the white and negro races ... That white persons are prohibited from sitting in or using any part of seating arrangements and sanitary or other facilities set apart for members of the negro race. That Negro persons are prohibited from sitting in or using any part of seating arrangements and sanitary or other facilities set apart for white persons.

In 1967 J. Edgar Hoovers FBI launched a discredit, disrupt, and destroy operation targeting Civil Rights Groups and Black Leaders labeled ***Subversive*** by Hoover. According to an actual memo from the head office of the FBI their mission was to expose, disrupt, misdirect and or ***neutralize*** subversive African Americans, which one could take that word as to mean Assassinate. This operation was conducted on African American Citizen and still is to this day, but we are only fighting for our civil rights and to be treated equal. Hoovers FBI conducted illegal break ins, one break in was into the office of The Southern Christian Leadership Conference which was a civil rights organization founded in 1957 which help stage the 381-day boycott of the Montgomery Alabama bus system and founded by Dr. Martin Luther King. Hoover made numerous attempts to what was known in the bureau as ***Neutralizing,*** and

Hoover made it a task to neutralizing black leaders. On April 4th, 1968, the day of the assassination of Dr. King. It was rumored that in the Alabama Office of the FBI agents where heard cheering and stating words to the effects of "***We*** finally got the son of a bitch!" **We?** It has now been brought to the fore front that the Government was involved in the killing of Malcom X. One of the reasons Hoover tasks was so determined to neutralize black leaders is the fact he did not want a ***Black Messiah*** to rally African Americans. It leaves one to believe that any attempt by African Americans in this country to free ourselves is literally a threat to national security and this country and every attempt we make we are dealt with the same way. The United States Government has conducted and is continuing their operation against African American Citizen the same way they are conducting operation against the foreign threats outside of this country. Yes, we are a ***threat.***

Chapter 3

Chemical Warfare

During the first World War chemical weapons were used against the enemy to incapacitate or kill them. Now dangerous chemicals are used on the civilian populations by the hundreds of thousands. In aerial sprays, liquids, and vectors. In military grade chemical there are 2 types, persistent agents, and non-persistent agents. Non-persistent agents have an effectiveness anywhere from a couple's hours to a few days. Non-persistent agents are basically use when the military wants to hinder the enemy temporarily with the intent to take over and or occupy the enemy territory. Persistent agents are designed to remain with the intent to permanently damage and or kill the enemy and their territory. We have a planet that contains thousands of dangerous and hazardous chemicals. In the air, food, and water. Chemicals that are used in the water and food that we consume and the air we breathe.

Now we have children with respiratory problems from air pollution. Lead and mercury in the water, steroids, and growth hormones in the meat our children consume. Server-side effects from the medications our Doctors prescribe.

Yet we cannot understand why our children are suffering from aggressive behavior, headaches, irritability, loss of developmental skills, memory loss and a low IQ and learning difficulties. Lead is a persistent chemical agent that has been found in water, paints and even treated wood in our homes. Other banned chemicals are Red Dye #40, Yellow Dye #5 Yellow Dye #6. Yellow Dye #5 and #6 are commonly used in some processed food and drinks to look pleasing to the eyes of the consumer. These chemicals are banned in other countries throughout the world but are still being used in the United States. Their used in everything from Mac and Cheese to Dog Food, some of these colorings are made from coal tar, yes ***COAL TAR***. The same coal tar that is also used to make and or manufacture products like floor polish and Head Lice shampoos. What about some of the fat free products you ask?

You must be asking about Olestra which is used in fat free potato chips as a fat substitute. By the way, the United Kingdom and Canada have banned the use of this substitute.

Then there is BHA and BHT. Both chemicals are ***Phenolic.***

Now Webster's Dictionary says:

: A usually thermosetting resin or plastic made by condensation of a phenol with an aldehyde and used especially for molding and insulating and in coatings and adhesives.

— called also phenolic resin

BHA Characteristics

- BHA is a mixture of the isomers 3-*tert*-butyl-4-hydroxyanisole and 2-*tert*-butyl-4-hydroxyanisole. Also known as BOA, *tert*-butyl-4-hydroxyanisole, (1,1-dimethylethyl)-4-methoxyphenol, *tert*-butyl-4-methoxyphenol, antioxyne B, and under various trade names
- Molecular formula $C_{11}H_{16}O_2$
- White or yellowish waxy solid
- Faint characteristic aromatic odor

BHT Characteristics

- Also known as 3,5-di-*tert*-butyl-4-hydroxytoluene; methyl-di-*tert*-butyl phenol; 2,6-di-*tert*-butyl-*para*-cresol
- Molecular formula $C_{15}H_{24}O$
- White powder

This same chemical that is found in butter and meats. They are also found in our rubber products, cosmetics, and food packaging. The National Institute of Health found the BHA may be a cancer-causing carcinogen. Another additive that is used in breads and frozen dinners is Azodicarbonamide. US food companies use this chemical to bleach flour even though flour naturally turns white on its own after a few weeks. Another chemical classified as a carcinogen is ***Arsenic*** which has been banned by the EU (European Union) since 1999, is still being used in the US in chicken feed to promote growth. rBGH and rBST. rBGH ***(Recombinant Bovine Somatotropin)*** also known as Posilac, a synthetic growth hormone given to cows to produce more milk and was created by Monsanto, yes can you say ***Roundup Weed Killer.*** And yes, this chemical is also banned in 27 countries. Since then, 1/3 of U.S. Cows have been injected with this chemical. In the 1980's. In 1997 Monsanto filed a lawsuit against WTVT (Channel 13) in

Tampa Florida when the Network was about to air a segment reveling that the rBGH that was being injected into the cows was being passed through the milk being consumed by humans. Monsanto was able to pull the segment before it aired and buried it.

Another Chemical used by some soft drink makers is BVO (Brominated vegetable oil) used in sports drinks to keep the flavoring from floating to the top of the beverage. High levels of this BVO made lead to hypothyroidism, autoimmune disorders, and cancer. The vaccines that were given to our children on a yearly basis have been found to contain Aluminum, Formaldehyde, MSG, and Thimerosal commonly known as Mercury.

There is even PFOS (Perfluoroctanesulfonic) that is used in household cleaning products i.e., Scotchgard, a fabric protector manufactured by 3M. This same PFOS is also used as the sodium or potassium salts. Environmental Directorate conducted a study that showed that PFOS is a persistent and toxic to humans and wildlife. The brand ***Posilac*** was brought by Eli Lilly Co in the 1980's. The same Eli Lilly that created the suicidal anti-depressant Prozac. It is also used in Textiles, paper, leather, paints, and polishes. Once these chemicals get into your blood it is there to stay.

The thing that is funny is this false idea that these same hazardous chemicals are safe in low doses. There is also the high chance of once exposed to these chemicals that it gets past to our unborn children in the form of birth defects. There is also the chemical chlorine which has been known to cause problems in the brain and even possibly dementia. Chlorine is also found in household cleaners and swimming pools. It has been also known to cause asthma in swimmers who have been exposed over periods of time and will cause eyes and skin irritation. Then there is everyone's favorite, ***Fluoride***. This compound is found in tap water and in tooth paste and mouth wash. There has always been a dispute regarding the safety of fluoride in drinking water and toothpaste. Some reports stated that fluoride was safe and there have been others condemning the use and or long-term use of fluoride. The one thing no one wants to mention is Dental Fluorosis. Believe it or not this is a common disorder, characterized by hypo mineralization to tooth enamel cause by consuming large amounts of fluoride during enamel formation.

There have been secret experiments sanctioned by the United States Government has either used directly or sponsored someone and or a company to use dangerous and hazardous chemicals on African Americans. In March of 1945 Ebb Cade was involved in a traffic accident in Tennessee and was transported to Oak Ridge Hospital with multiple fractures. While in the hospital he became known as HP-12 (Human Product 12). On April 10, 1945 Dr. Friedell began injecting Cade with Plutonium. This test was to determine the migration of Plutonium through the body. During the test, 15 teeth where extracted and bone samples were taken. From 1945 thru 1947 a total of 18 subjects where tested.

11 Patients in Strong Memorial Hospital in Rochester, New York.

3 Patients in Billings Hospital in Chicago Illinois.

3 Patients in University Hospital in San Francisco, California.

Albert Stevens, a test subject/patient was given 10x the amount while being tested he is urine and feces samples were taken and sent to Los Alamos for Plutonium analysis. He later died of cancer.

Dr. Albert Kligman

Between 1965 thru 1966 one Dr. Albert Kligman a well-known Dermatologist, also inventor of Retin-A skin cream. Exposed black prisoners to dioxin. The main ingredient to the well-known military weapon Agent Orange the same agent which was created and manufactured by Dow Chemicals. This continued until the 1976 DHEW Report was released stating the amounts of chemicals called for where minimal at best but resulted in many of the inmates having volcanic eruptions of chloracne, which were a severe combination of blackheads, cysts pustules on the face, armpits, and groin area. Dr. Kligman continued his weapons testing on African America prisoners in 1996 on Holmesburg Prison in Philadelphia. Other test that where supervised or conducted by Kligman performed on Black Prisoners. The chosen 468 black inmates were injected with a radioactive compound and or Hallucinogenic. Other biological experiments were conducted as well such as exposing black inmates to herpes complex and vaccinia virus. These painful side effects continued well after the experiments were over. Even with the Nuremburg Code, created in 1947, after World War II. In response of Nazi human experiments which banned such studies, yet the United States Government continued to support and fund these experiments on blacks. This is the norm, Government backed experiments on prisoners who are predominately

Black, who are volunteered for these horrific experiments with no compensation. Without having the right to sign a waiver or be allowed to refuse testing or granted relieve for their pain and suffering. This like many cases of where blacks are treated like lab rats. Klingmans research was Non-Therapeutic nor benefited human subjects, yet he was still supported and back by academic institutions and private companies.

.

James Marion Sims

Credited as being a pioneer in modern gynecology and for the development of tools and surgical techniques in the field of women's reproductive health and lionized with a half a dozen statues around the country praising his work for cutting into black enslaves women during the 19th century. Sims experimented on black enslaved women who had a condition known then as ***Fistulas***, now known as ***Crohn's Disease***. These procedures conducted on enslaved black women without anesthesia. Again, another act against an African Americans that never make the American History books. Sims, born in Lancaster South Carolina in 1813.

Entered the medical field never making it past internship and taking a 12-month course at Jefferson Medical College. Sims opened his practice in Montgomery Alabama with his first two patients dying at his hands. Even after their deaths Sims still managed to build a strong practice with white slave owners by treating their enslaved workers. During his examinations he would have the slave women get on all fours placing his hands inside their vagina. I am sure even back then the Veterinarians treated farm animals more humanely. Yet he was labeled a trailblazer with statues erected in his name and has only been removed in 2018. Yet the American Government condemned the acts of Josef Mengele AKA the Angel of death. Who was a German SS Officer and physician during World War II who performed horrific deadly experiments on prisoners mostly without anesthesia and awake during the procedures. Defenders of Sims say he was simply a man of his time for whom the end justified the means. Sims also conducted medical procedures on black enslaved children at times using a shoehorn during the procedures on the children.

Now where am I going with all this? I am trying to get to the point of Eugenics, Sterilization and Depopulation of African Americans.

Eugenics: *as defined in the Webster Dictionary*

- : the practice or advocacy of controlled selective breeding of human populations (as by sterilization) to improve the population's genetic composition, in 1883 Francis Galton, in England, coined the term "eugenics" to encompass the idea of modification of natural selection through selective breeding for the improvement of humankind ....

Racial Eugenics was a tactic used in the 40's and 60's and is still being used against African American Women. When the Chicago based Planned Parenthood, Association held Coffee get together on Birth Control in predominantly black section of Chicago but not one held in all white sections. Pittsburgh based Family Planning Programs went into the homes of predominantly black women to convince them to go onto birth control. For the women who refused they were threatened to have their government assistants cut off. When this attempted genocide was brought to the fore front the Office of Economic Opportunity's federal funds were cut off and it was also found that same OEO had funded 1000's of involuntary sterilization of black women in the south from the 1940's and 1950's. That same year Judges in New York where also threatening black women with forced birth control or have government assistants cut off.

At the moment, it is probable that the indirect effect of civilization is dysgenic instead of eugenic; and in any case it seems likely that the dead weight of genetic stupidity, physical weakness, mental instability, and disease-proneness, which already exist in the human species, will prove too great a burden for real progress to be achieved.

– Julian Huxley. UNESCO: Its Purpose and Its Philosophy, 1946.[1]

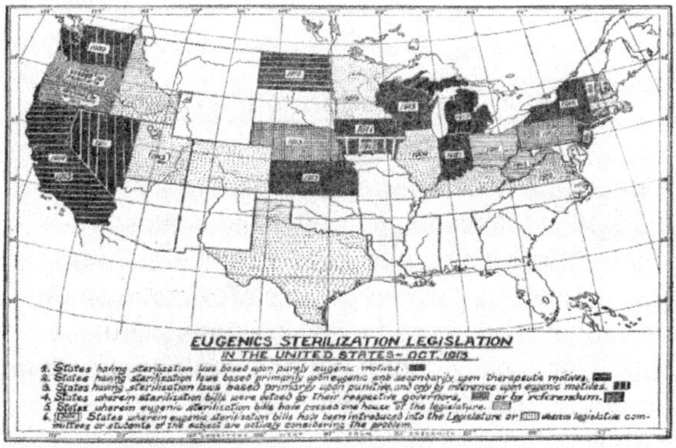

Blacks, Indigenous people, poor whites, and people with disabilities, became targets of eugenics programs.

Sterilization:

1909-1979: 20,000 Operations Performed in California

In a 70-year period, California performs a third of all government funded sterilizations in the United States. The practice largely targets Latinos and Blacks, and lead to a 1975 class-action lawsuit by working class Mexican women who were coerced into the procedure sometimes minutes after giving birth. California's continued and central role in the sterilization programs of the 20th century is highlighted by Dr. Alexandra Stern in "Sterilized in the name of Public Health: Race, Immigration and Reproductive Control in Modern California" (2005). In the article, Dr. Stern writes that Mexican-Americans and African Americans were disproportionally represented in the percentages of sterilization, and that this was rationalized by concerns about bad parenting, population burdens and even as "a punishment for bearing illegitimate children or as extortion to ensure ongoing receipt of family assistance (in the 1950s and 1960s)."

Depopulation:

"Maybe I am not objective when it comes to Planned Parenthood, but, you know, I know who Margaret Sanger is, and I know that she believed in eugenics, and that she was not particularly enamored with black people.

"And one of the reasons you find most of their clinics in black neighborhoods is so that you can find a way to control that population. I think people should go back and read about Margaret Sanger who founded this place – a woman Hillary Clinton by the way says that she admires. Look and see what many people in Nazi Germany thought about her."

Dr. Ben Carson

There is a term used today that really does not get any attention. That term is ***Environmental Racism.*** This is when a certain minority group is exposed to hazards chemicals as well as toxic waste and pollutants. There is not really any government regulation to deal with this issue and to prevent toxic material from being poured, dumped, or stored in areas that are inhabited by predominately people of color. Take Flint Michigan for example. Statistics show more African American live in environmentally unsafe housing, schools, playgrounds, and other facilities. Statistics also show black children are 5X more likely to have lead in the body than Caucasian children.

It seems that the Flint Michigan incident has brought all this to the fore front, but unfortunately before Flint there was the case of the Genesee Power Station. In 1995, also in Flint Michigan was an incinerator power station operated by a company name Genesee Power. This plant was also constructed not far from an elementary school for predominately black children. This plant was used to burn lead treated wood from demolished "Crack Houses".

The plant produced lead, carbon monoxide and nitrogen smoke. Before Genesee Power Station in 1966 there was Buick City. A 235-acre factory built by GM which produced thick cloud of carcinogenic smoke near Flint's poverty stricken predominately black neighborhoods. Native American land has been used as a dump for radioactive nuclear waste. There are other Flints across the U.S. Chicago, West, and South sides. Baltimore, East and North Baltimore. New Jersey.

Toxic Colonialism, it has been defined as the process by which underdeveloped states are used as inexpensive alternatives for the export or disposal of hazardous waste by developed states. There is also the ***"Global Waste Trade"*** this is an international agreement between countries to have waste moved to underdeveloped countries like Africa, Asian and Latin America and now America has become a major dumping ground for hazardous and very dangerous toxic material. As of 2017 there are more than 1300 hazard waste sites in America. Toxic waste site is always near highly populated areas New Jersey having the greatest number of sites with California and Pennsylvania close behind.

Chapter 4

Psychological Warfare and Mind Control

"Music directly imitates the passions or state of the soul; hence, when one listens to music that imitates certain passion, he becomes imbued with the same passion; ... In short, if one listens to the wrong kind of music, he will become the wrong kind of person; but conversely, if he listens to the right kind of music, he will tend to become the right kind of person."

-Aristotle

Mind Control, also known as Brain Washing and is commonly now called Conversion. Psychological Warfare also dates to the Second World War and you could also include propaganda. The practice of mind control has been going since time in remembrance. It comes in many forms, drugs, music, torture, propaganda. It has always worked on those who were followers or weak minded. Hitler was able to gain control and rule over German simply by catching the people of German at a weak moment in their lives when there was poverty and depression. It was then he was able to rally the people with his words and showed the people how to project the people's anger on their enemies.

We are in an era where we are bombarded with music that is graphic in nature and violence in video games and movies, and now let us add onto this so-called Reality Television. We all know that Reality Television is not really ***REALITY.*** No one dresses like that, no one acts like that. But we are led to believe that this is the new norm. In the current Hip-Hop Social Media Culture there are prominent figures that project an image. It is an image of drug dealing weed smoking, womanizing Gang Banging and straight up killing. These images a burned into the thought process of our young black children. Music video after music video of young black men jumping around wearing gold pushing nice cars and young girls in the background in bikini and thongs twerking and shaking. This along with the subliminal music leads young black men into that life. The life of displaying Anti-Social behavior not only in school but in the public and at home with their own parents. Anti-Social behavior with those in authority. The Teacher, Law Enforcement Officers, the Mother, and the Father. The Social

Studies Teacher whom children use to have some much respect for and now teachers are getting physically assaulted all most daily. The 5-year-old that went from yelling "Hi Police!" to yelling "Fuck the Police!" The yelling and cursing at the mothers and fathers by the now 15-year-old. Gone are the day of Curtis Blow and the Sugar Hill Gang rapping about being a Ladies Man and being cool. Unfortunately, they believe what they see on the music video as real life. Live a life of a thug and you can have the money, cars, and women and the Hip Hop culture have turned the Street Thug into a hero. These video and reality shows have young girls thinking the same way. Dress like this and act like a ratchet street Whore. Wear the long fake hair down to her waist, wear the skirt up to her butt cheeks. Sport their long fake nails that are so long the look like claws. When it comes to mind control one of the best methods is music. Music has great power and control over someone's thought processes. Now you might think I have no idea what I am talking about but think about what I am saying about the powerful music and its affect your emotions and thought process.

For those who love Gospel music, think about how that makes you feel and how that Gospel music moves you in a positive way, full of joy and the Holy Spirit. Think about Jazz music. How it makes you feel chill and relaxed. How R&B puts one in a romantic mood. Rock music during a sports game or action movie. It puts our mind in a certain perspective. How Rap music makes you want to dance and Rap along with the song because you know the lyrics by heart. The lyrics. Queens "We are the Champions" is sung during just about every game victory.

Every time I hear Wagner's ***"Ride of the Valkyries"*** I think about the scene from **Apocalypse Now** of attack Helicopters flying in to kill the enemy. My point is whether you believe it or not, there is music out there that can make you happy, it can make you sad, and it could put you in to a state of mind that might have you do violence. Certain owners of the music label produce music i.e., Rap with certain types of lyrics. If you listen to certain types of Rap that promote acts of violence when they Rap about "Busting a cap in a Nigga's ass" or having sex with a THOT they met at the Club.

Let us not leave out Rock music. On July 2, 1991 during a Guns N Roses concert in St. Louis Missouri a large crowd of 2500 youth staged a riot injuring 60 people. Jefferson-Township New Jersey, a youth named Thomas Sullivan stabbed his mother to death and attempted to kill the rest of his family.

Once he was caught by the Police, he had admitted listening to hard metal Rock music and Satan appeared to him and told him to kill his family. So, this does leave open the question, can music manipulate one's mind and or behavior?

Other versions of mind control are what was called back during the first and Second World War as Propaganda. This is done by transmitting and or communicating information that is used to influence and further an agenda, this was also used to promote an emotional rather that rational responses to the information given. Propaganda was first used by the military and prepared by the military but now activist groups, companies', religious organizations, and the media produce propaganda.

During the 20th century the meaning of propaganda is associated with a manipulative approach, different materials are used to convey propaganda messages. In 1929, a well-known literary Everett Dean Marin argues that propaganda is making puppets of us.

"We are moved by hidden strings which the propagandist manipulates."

Everett Dean Marin

Czech historian Defined propaganda as either white, grey, or black.

White- Openly disclosed.

Grey- Ambiguous or non-disclosed source.

Black- Published by the enemy.

Wartime propaganda is a powerful weapon used to dehumanize and create hatred toward a supposed enemy. By creating a false image in the mind of others using derogatory or racist terms. The most vulnerable targets for propaganda are children. Propaganda in schools began in Germany during the 1930's through the 1940's. Today the standard media used to disseminate propaganda is News Reports, Government reports, books, movies, radio and via a website. U.S. Law Enforcement uses a variety of tactics and dirty tricks to sabotage certain movements. They use false media stories and leaflets and phone calls, fake documents they use what is called bad jacking to create an air of suspicion.

Others forms of mind control comes also in the form of Pharmaceuticals. The concept of using drugs to aid in controlling one's mind has been going on since time in remembrance. LSD is one of the best-known drugs used in mind control. It is known that even the Military used LSD on subject during mind control experiments. Other known drugs...

Chlorpromazine (Thorazine) – Schizophrenia

Pipradrol- ADHD

Ritalin-ADHD

Adderall-ADHD

Ritalin is the current drug used for children with ADHD. Ritalin is a highly potent narcotic known as a Class 2 and regulated by the DEA. Ritalin stimulate the central nervous system. The side effects include....

Sudden Death-Stroke-Heart Attack-High Blood Pressure-Behavior Problems-Aggressive Behavior-Psychotic Symptom including hearing voice.

Adderall is another drug used for children with ADHD this medication is a combination of

Amphetamine and Dextroamphetmine. The side effects include...

Hostility-Behavior Problems- Psychotic Behavior including hearing voices.

Part of the problem of some of these medications is the side effects are worse than the condition. Some of these ADHD medications have been known to bring on suicidal tendencies and now there are cases where the child has been missed diagnosed. There is a 70% increase in ADHD among black children, study finds and 90% of those are black girls. The problem steams that a large majority of black children are miss diagnosed. Some of those children could be suffering from trauma such as violence, physical abuse and or PTSD.

It is believed that a lot of the miss diagnoses steams from poorly trained teachers on handling off-task behaviors. Black children are being recommended at great numbers to be prescribed highly dangerous psychotic substances that is not the cure to their behavior but only to sedate them. There are parents who are not opting to place the children on any ADHD medications or behavior altering medications, and yes that seems to come with a problem as well.

There are parents who are being criminally charged for refusal to place their children on behavior medications and for those who take their children off these medications. There have been cases where CPS (Child Protective Services) has taken children from the homes of parent who refuse to medicate their children who are diagnosed with a behavior disorder.

A teacher called CPS after seeing self-inflicted scratches on a 17-year-old Autistic boy named Nate and notified CPS and filed a complaint regarding a Doctor approved arm restraint to keep him from hurting himself the Government took the boy CPS placed him in a group home where he ran away. CPS then placed him in a mental Hospital where Staff had placed him on drugs that caused Grand Mal seizures when his parents visited him his face was swollen, and he was in and out of consciousness and suffered from convulsions. His Physician, Dr. Mercola stated

"What kind of society rips a 17-year-old autistic boy from his loving home and place him in a state-run metal institution where he is given heavy doses of drugs kept physically restrained, kept away from his family, deprived of books and other mental stimulation and is left alone to rot?"

Conclusions

One cannot help but to think that all this that is going on here in America against the African American is nothing but hate, bigotry and racism on a level never seen. Our continent, Africa was invaded by an armed militia. Our men and women were taken in chains as captives of this invasion as prisoners of this race war. We were held as prisoners of war as African people are placed into concentration camps called plantations now known as prisons and forced to work in these labor camps. Sadly, this war. This 400-year war on African Americans is still being fought across the Nation. This violence war continues against African American has casualties, so many that it had a name, ***Race Massacres***.

The Rosewood massacre of 1923

In the beginning Rosewood was a town predominately of both black and white. By 1890 and the pencil mills had shut down, many white residents relocated to Sumner. By 1900 Rosewood had become predominately black. By 1915 the population of Rosewood had reached 350 people. Also, by the 1900's Florida had implemented legal racial segregation under the Jim Crow Laws which mandated that blacks and whites remained separate in public facilities and on transportation. By 1920 Rosewood had become self-sufficient with their own churches, schools and a turpentine and sugarcane mill.

It was January 1923 the town of Rosewood was destroyed by race riots. This stemming from a group of white men who Lynch a black resident of Rosewood who was accused of assaulting a white woman in nearby Sumner. A mob of over 100 white men invaded Rosewood and left a wake of destruction. Survivor had to hide in the swamps until they were able to escape the mob. When it was over approximately 27 blacks were killed.

The Tulsa massacre of 1921

On May 3, 1921, a white mob, armed and deputized by Government officials launched a 2- day attack against the black residences and business owners of Tulsa Oklahoma. Reports read that armed white men shot and killed blacks as they attempted to flee. Black owned homes and businesses were burned to the ground and what was not burned was raided and looted. During the attacks it was also reported that private planes, flown by white men were flying over Tulsa firing from the air and dropping bombs on the black population.

This attack was called by many the worse incident of racial violence in America. After it was all said and done an estimated 39 African Americans where dead and another estimated 800 where hospitalized, another 10,000 were left homeless with the property damage value in the millions. How did this massacre start on what was supposed to be a Memorial Day weekend? It started when Sarah Page, a white 17- year- old elevator operator of the Drexel Building accused Dick Rowland, black 19- year- old shoe shiner of assaulting her. Rowland was arrested. As Rowland sat in jail rumor traveled though Tulsa that a large group of white men were about to go to the jail and Lynch Rowland. It was then approximately 75 black men armed themselves and headed to the jail in hopes to keep Rowland from being Lynch by the white mob. Reports read that there was an armed standoff between both groups and that the Sheriff was able to de-escalate the situation. It was then, as reported. A white man allegedly attempted to disarm one of the black men. A shot rang out. It was that point stated the Sheriff "All hell broke loose!"

A shootout between the two groups which left 10 white men dead and 2 blacks. Mob violence erupted which by the morning left Tulsa burnt to the grown. Prior to that day Greenwood, which was a district in Tulsa. Was organized and formed by Booker T. Washington in 1906. The Greenwood District had become so prosperous that had become to be known as Black Wall Street.

The 16th St. Baptist Church bombing

Before it was labeled ***Domestic Terrorism***. On September 15th, 1963. 4 members of the Alabama Klu Klux Klan planted 19 sticks of explosives rigged with a timing device under the steps of the church of 16th St. Baptist Church. By 10:22 AM approximately 14 people were injured, and four young black girls were dead.

Addie Mae Collins- Age 14

Carol Denise McNair- Age 11

Carole Rosanond Robertson- Age 14

Cynthia Dionne Wesley- Age 14

Their bodies where so mutilated that that they were identified by their clothing and Jewelry. This caused an unrest throughout the city, as the church bombing made national and international news. It was also report that white supremacists celebrated the bombing and the killing as "***Four less niggers***." Even hours after 4 young girls lay dead in the bombing debris, two more lives where taken. Johnny Robinson, age 16 and Virgil Ware, age 13. Robinson was shot in the back by Police as he fled the scene of a group of blacks who were allegedly throwing rocks at vehicles passing by. Ware was blatantly shot by Larry Sims, a white 16. Sims was convicted of second-degree manslaughter, but a judge found it fitting to give him 2 years' probation. The FBI Investigators had suspects in the case, but the investigation was hindered by J. Edger Hoover himself and the reports were sealed also by order of J. Edger Hoover.

The Lynching and murder of 14-year-old Emmet Till

During the summer of August 1955, a 14-year-old black boy from Chicago named Emit Till was visiting family in Money Mississippi. While on his summer vacation he happened to meet and speak with a 21-year-old Carolyn Bryant. It was this encounter that would open this countries eyes to true racial hate and how truly violent Lynch was of blacks in America.

After several days after Emmitt's encounter with Bryant, 2 armed white men, Roy Bryant, and J. W. Milam. Would take Emmet from his Uncle's home, taken to an unknown location where he would be beaten then shot in the head and his mutilated body was found in the Tallahatchie River 3 days later. His body was returned to Chicago in which his mother, Mamie Carthan Till, demanded a public funeral, which was held at the Roberts Temple Church of God in Christ in which tens of thousands attended. After Bryant and Milam were found not guilty, they publicly admitted to killing Till. Carolyn Bryant years later admitted that she lied about what happen and was never charged or convicted.

The Assassination of Medgar Evers

It is June 12th, 1963, Jackson Tennessee. A man was exiting his vehicle about to enter his home, when a bullet, from 10 meters away strikes him in the back. He manages to make it 30 feet to his home were his wife found him and got him to a hospital. Unfortunately, he dies almost an hour later after reaching the hospital. Not by the gunshot wound, but the fact that the victim was black. That black man was 37- year- old Medgar Evers. A World War II Veteran, Evers not only fought in the War but fought against segregation in the United States.

His Assassin, Byron De La Beckwith. A member of the White Citizens Council and later a member of the KKK. Beckwith shot and killed Evers with a 1917 Rifle commonly used in combat. Beckwith was eventually acquitted by an all-white jury. Prior to his assassination Evers had FBI, and Police Security because of the threats on his life. Unfortunately, the morning of his Assassination no security was present. There were those who believed that there where members of the KKK within the Police Department.

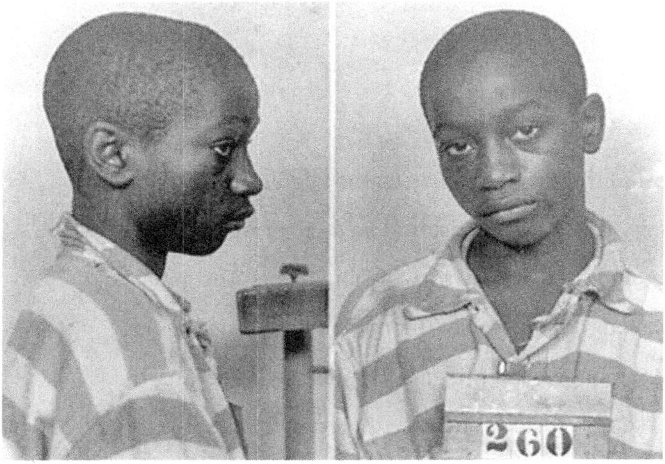

The Execution of George Stinney

It is June 16th, 1944, the time is 7:30 PM in a South Carolina prison. An inmate was preparing for execution by electric chair for the double murder of 2 little white girls. Betty June Binnicker, age 11 and Mary Emma Thames, age 7. Both found in a ditch just outside of the predominately black side of Alcolu, South Carolina. They had gone missing for almost 2 days, both suffering from blunt force trauma to the head and face but no sign of sexual assault.

It was reported the girls were seen by the Stinney property the day before asking George and his sister Aime do they know where they can find ***Maypops*** better known as Passionflowers. The initial investigation led to the arrest of George Stinney Jr and his older brother John. John was later released for unknown reasons, but George was kept in custody and was not allowed to see his parents until after his conviction.

In a statement by Clarendon County Deputy H. S. Newman, Stinney had made a full confession to the double murder and took the police to where the murder weapon was kept by Stinney, even though no official written statement was ever given by or signed by Stinney. Stinney later stated that he made the alleged verbal confession because police were starving Stinney and bribing him with food. Other violations of Stinney's constitutional rights were Stinney being question without his parents being present. Stinney's court appointed attorney was a tax commissioner Charles Plowden. During trial Plowden never cross examined the Officers on their interrogation of Stinney.

During the one-day trial the courtroom was packed with approximately 1000 whites. No blacks were allowed in the courtroom. After the juries 10-minute deliberation. George Stinney was found guilty of the murder of both girls at which time Judge Phillip H. Stoll Sentenced 14-year-old George Stinney Jr to death by electrocution. During his preparation for electrocution a Bible had to be placed under him as a buster seat because he was so small. Stinney body was placed in an unmarked grave in Crowley.

The Assassination of Fred Hampton

On December 4th, 1969, the Chicago Police Department and the FBI conducted a predawn raid on the apartment of Fred Hampton. When it was over 90 rounds had been fired and Hampton and Mark Clark were dead. During an inquest, a jury found that the death of Hampton, who was drugged and killed in his bed during the raid justifiable homicide. Prior to his murder, Hampton was an activist and a chairman of the Illinois chapter of the Black Panther Party. Also known as a Political organizer that included the Black Panthers, and the Young Patriots.

Hampton was also able to form an alliance for a truce with the street gangs to end infighting and to work on social change.
In 1967 the FBI identified Hampton as a threat. The FBI also made numerous attempts to discredit and subvert his activity through out Chicago and infiltrating the Chicago based Black Panthers. With his ability to bring people and organization together the FBI considered Hampton a major threat so much that J. Edgar Hoover was Hell bent on stopping the major formation of the Panther, Young Patriots and Young Lords from becoming a major coalition in Chicago which would result in a revolution that could cause a major up rising among African Americans. Fear of this revolution was so great that the FBI Senate investigations showed.

The FBI encouraged violence between the Panther Party and other radical groups which resulted in murders throughout the country. An armed shootout between radical party members and the Chicago Police resulted in on Black Panther Party member mortally wounded and the arrest of 6 others.

The Assassination of Malcom X

The day in history which I believed signed the death warrant for Malcom X. April 26th, 1957 NYPD attempted to arrest Reece Poe. As he was being beaten to the ground resisting, the assault was interrupted by Johnson Hinton. Hinton yelled "You're not in Alabama! This is New York!" The Police then turned their attention to Hinton. Hinton was arrested without being treated for his injuries he received after his arrest. When word reached Malcom X and the Nation of Islam,

Malcom rallied several hundred men that marched on the 28th precinct on West 123 St. to petition Hinton's release. Hinton was finally transported to Harlem Hospital as protesters followed. Once treated, Hinton was transported by NYPD back to the precinct where he continued to be held. NYPD Deputy Inspector McGowan was able to get James Hicks, a friend of Malcom X, to attempt to mediate between Malcom X and NYPD to defuse the situation. Upon Hicks arrival to the precinct over 1000 Nation of Islam members had gathered. Out numbering the Police, On April 27th Hinton was released on bail, paid by the Nation of Islam, and taken to the Sydenham Hospital in Harlem. This incident-imposed fear in the NYPD and the FBI. The fear was a thousand disciplined black men appearing on the order of one man,

Malcom X. No black man should have such power. Malcom X was J. Edgar Hoovers ***Black Messiah***. One of Hoovers biggest fears. On February 21st, 1965 while standing at the podium giving his speech to the Organization of Afro-American Unity, being held at the Audubon Ballroom in Harlem. An infiltrator of the Nation of Islam open fire on Malcom X. He would succumb to his injuries. Just as Medgar Evers, Malcom X security was not present as there would normally be.

The Charlestown Church massacre of 2015

On June 17th, 2015 at a church in South Carolina, the members have gathered for bible study. Enter Dylann Roof, a known White Supremist and Neo Nazi walks in during the members bible study. At 8:16 PM Dylann entered a side door armed with a Glock 41 .45 Cal handgun. 6 minutes later 9 people would be dead. His reason for the shooting? That black men were coming to rape white women and take over the country. His last words where ***"If you're going pray, I'm going to give you something to pray about."***

The Ocoee Massacre 1920 Florida

The **Ocoee massacre** was one of the most violent massacres in United States history. But then again, every massacre against black Americans have been called the most violent massacres which would lead one to believe with all the massacres in the United States one was just as or worst than the last. But this one was no different than any other massacre in America against blacks. All of them involved the killing of African Americans and the burning of their homes and businesses. This massacre, November 2, 1920. Which resulted in the deaths of 35 blacks.

This was stemming from the right to vote. The simple act of blacks trying to exercise their constitutional right to vote turned into an all-out massacre of those blacks. Mose Norman, who was one of Ocoee prosperous farmers. Norman who attempted to vote and was turned away. Norman was also one of those who was leading the voter drive. An armed white mob formed around the home of Julius Perry, where the mob believed Norman as staying. Perry, to defend himself. Opened fire killing 2. Word of the shooting caused more white men to respond from neighboring Orland and Orange County. This resulted in the devastation of northern Ocoee.

The white mob found Perry attempting to flee Ocoee. His body was found hanging from a telephone near the highway with a sign that read ***"This is what we do to niggers that vote".*** The lynch mob, who was led by the former police chief of Orlando, Sam Salisbury called for the man hunt of Norman, but he was never found. One of the many casualties was Langmaid, a black carpenter. Who was found beaten and castrated. The mob had driven approximately 500 blacks from Ocoee leaving it predominantly white. The FBI was sent in to investigate possible election fraud. No investigation was ever conducted regarding the murders of the black residence or the arson of their homes.

Yet African Americans are always expected by the US Government and by even some of our African American leaders to be forgiven and a peaceful people. This urban war is killing our people by the thousand at the hands of the paramilitary army known as Law Enforcement. This war will continue, it will continue without a victor, without a truce, or a surrender. So, let us try to understand something that is totally not possible to understand. We, Americans of African descent are at war with a violent race. Now I investigated the brief history of Americas white Aryan race, which was born of people in the India European region, i.e., people of color. Then used by Adolph Hitler in his myth of the pure Aryan race and make it his own believe, German Aryans who were born in the time of Hitler had to prove their Aryan heritage through their blood line. We are at war with race that can be considered narcissistic by clinical standards. A race that is prejudice, racism, and bigotry.

Let us break this down because these words have different meanings but are in the same category.

Prejudice: **Preconceived opinion that is not based on reason or actual experience**

Racism: **policies, behavior's, rules, etc. that result in a continued unfair advantage to**

some people and unfair or harmful treatment of others based on r ace

Bigotry:The fact ofhavingand expressing strong, unreasonable beli efs and disliking other

People who have different beliefs or a different way of life

This feeling all stemming from a fear, a fear of not knowing African Americans. That is one of the reasons why white racists feel the constant need to dominate. There is always this need to dominate and control everything. It is said that those that feel a need to dominate are reacting to a point of weakness, they continue in a pursuit of control, to dominate others to ease their rears of inevitable extinction. I say extinction because there is more inter racial children now then even which means there will be less and less pure blood whites and or Aryans in this country.

Let us not forget to insert hate in this chapter as well. Hate which the real reason all of this is happening. Many Psychologists feel the reason why we hate is that we are searching for the source or cause of the emotion of fear, rage and resentment and we turn the emotion onto a person or persons and project that emotion onto someone else as a defense mechanism that allows us to avoid facing their own shortcomings by transferring them onto to others. The person holding the hate believes on some deep feeling that they feel is true about themselves. The want to hate, they need to hate. So, in conclusions putting all chapters together, call me crazy or a conspiracy theorist but just look around you to see for yourself how the world is changing and not for the better. It is not changing for the better and it is not going to change for the better until we make a real stand against those who want to hold us down with

Racism and those who want to hold us down with the "Don't worry, we'll take care of you with our handouts and welfare programs". The day is near, and it is going to happen, why because we are walking around with our heads buried in our smart phone screens or watching an imaginary reality show. They know your either not paying attention or you just do not care. The sad part is the only time you will wake up and see what is going on will be the day when you gaze into the screen of that smart phone and see that the powers that have declared Marshall Law.

Made in the USA
Monee, IL
04 November 2026

67378026R00066